How To Find All Missing Persons / Unsolved Cases. And Collect All Reward Offers. Volume VI THE CASE OF CHRISTINE MARIE EASTIN

David Gomadza

www.twofuture.world

PAPERBACK **ISBN:** 9798325960604

DEDICATION

A better world.

CONTENTS

ACKNOWLEDGMENTS

Tomorrow's World Order

HOW TO FIND ALL MISSING PERSONS / UNSOLVED CASES AND COLLECT ALL REWARD OFFERS THE FORMULA VOLUME VI THE CASE OF CHRISTINE MARIE EASTIN

BACKGROUND INFORMATION

CHRISTINE MARIE EASTIN

January 18, 1971
Hayward, California

White

Details:

Christine Marie Eastin went missing from Hayward, California, on January 18, 1971. She left her home at 10:00 p.m. to go to the car wash and then pick up her friend at the local Jack in the Box restaurant. She never arrived to pick up her friend. The vehicle she drove was found at a car wash located at 25400 Mission Boulevard in Hayward. Her purse was locked inside the vehicle. Christine was last seen wearing a black/brown leather coat, black boots, blue slacks, a red, white, and blue pinstriped tunic, and a bluish gold scarf

TOMORROW'S WORD ORDER'S PRESPECTIVE

This is how we as Tomorrow's World Order solved this case with myself [David Gomadza] as the founder, and the president of the whole world. www.twofuture.world

All information on the website could be write and could be wrong most is totally different from our account in many respect writing my account I did not research anything on the internet so don't be surprised to find out what I am going to say is totally different from all these accounts.

I look at missing persons cases simply based on brain reading that means if I get right person's brain readings then this account is 100% accurate so far.

Signed

David Gomadza

00447719210295

Davidgomadza@hotmail.com

How To Find All Missing Persons / Unsolved Cases. And Collect All Reward Offers. Volume VI CHRISTINE MARIE EASTIN

Www.twofuture.world

THE FUTURE: THE AFTERLIFE CONVERSATION AND THE COUNCIL OF CREATION oh my god i died i was raped before i even open my mouth and died before i said anything and this is regarded as the most silent case in the history of the court of creation and the shortest of all time in the history of the court of appeal to decide on this is what happened in layman's terms i got in my car and said i can but then and got out then said can i but then what and got out of the car and went back inside now inside i pulled down my pants and literally put a finger in my pussy and said what if then i went inside the car and said what can be will be but then got out and went in the house and said what could be must be but then went back inside the house and when i come a car passed by and horned so hard i had a clit erection in ecstasy about what could be then i went to the toilet and fingers my arse for 1 minute actually checking the time and went out and started the car and drove off with a clit erection until i reached the town then other cars started horsing their vehicles and i deliberately started slowing down so that others horn me and literally the clit election died down and i forgot all about it and went inside jack and the box and got a big bucket of the most expensive food without the money to pay for it but said wait i left my purse in the car and walked out then a guy got up and said i can pay for you but and looked at my tits being a blond i know i was not endowed in that area so i said i can but and he smiled and said you are not bad yourself so who teach you the language of the gods surely it can't be the gods because you would not even look at me if it's were them i said it's their teachers who are teaching me that's why i can look at you and glorify them for making you look but i see he said well thought seriously who is teaching you and i said no one had a dream one day and started saying but all the time until everyone start calling me but but with at and instantly my clit erection got back harder than before and i said can i ask what you do he said teach to walk but after running and i looked perplexed and he said i can show you how and i said okay stop with a clit election and he said can you ask me any question but fast and i said can you swim but and he said but i can but but the first but was a butt i looked at him and said how face and he said for a wise girl and i said can we but then i stopped he instantly said bucket of jack at the box and i said can but and he said okay my house but and i said can wait but and he said you can but but and he said but but i am confused because but don't follow but unless and my heart tore when i realised what he had just said then he said unless you can but then he instantly touched my hand and said what could be and i said i minute if but he looked startled and said must be good for 1 minute but then he said okay if you say it can in 1 minute but and i looked lost thinking weighing all the options and said if one can then another must his reactions were what the fuck but then i said ready for you in men's cubicle toilet and he said i go first make0 sure no other can first not and then he walked backward so that i can see him and entered inside and i said ok i can tighten hard but then i waited about two minutes and then went in but ... woke up dead i cried hard but... now this is another case of misdemeanor where a woman trade life for needs if not wants one woman traded life for food with serious consequences a one horad blacksmith said i can play your game of the gods and cut you into two to match because it takes the average man 2 minutes to orgasm and i am going to set a record and prove it so so he get aroused really hard and waited then she did not come until 4 minutes later when hard on had subsided then it took 3 more minutes squeezing her boobs to put her off but also removing the arse rim that was to make it possible and if we can ask what can be of her then it can be done but all now knew that it might end up badly so the woman said rim now off but the he said deliberate delay but and she said takes minimum 2 minutes to so half already given but he looked like an idiot and said still learning but then again she said what chances now or but end he said wasting time again make even worse but she looked confused and said i can reschedule until perfect ready not in a rush but then he agreed realizing that this was his best option she realized that it was fair she honesty waited to give him time to wank then just come and be butted before he ejaculated now if we look at this case this is the most straight forward case ever because we have the same players from start until the end now lets look at the facts of the case she is hungry and wants the largest bucket of food for a dip in the butt hole but she is tight with time as her wish everything must happen within one minute but then again it's asking too much what can anyone do within one minute let's see how this unfolds now he looks at his time and say go to the door and back then count from minute it died in until i come and you can say 1,2,3,4,5,6,7 until 60 then that 1 minute now she said i want rim so i extra minute to be ready and he said fair so i count when 60 then 1 minute for rim now this is exactly what happened he said 1,2,3,4,5 and looked at her as she went then stopped because the male brain cannot count and prepare for sex so he stopped and started preparing and now she realised that that might have been the sending off so she slowly everything down a bit to make sure he gets at least 2 minutes then she said okay i come he remained quite woman who talk during sex and slapping so he raised hand and said only 10 left better be fast according to her 20 was left but only because she had slowed down things now as she looked at him he was reciting something over and over again and she was happy because she really wanted him to cum in a minute so she knelt down and said fuck me hard then she spread hard than he had imagined and for sure it took 30 strong animal strokes with a squirt on her part and he growled so loud that everyone in the restaurant heard that and laughed so hard that they literally said he cum half the time but this was not the issue the issue is that the food had gone cold double the time but he had not known anything about the food going cold that he looked really shocked and said why everyone is laughing and she said wit that loud cry who can't laugh try it again and hear it this time even louder seriously he tried and stopped in the middle and laughed and said i guess you teach the gods and they all laugh but then she said okay let's go for a round of applause for being the first who let but then who cares if you are but and stopped he looked confused realizing that the laugh was about something so he said i go first and said she run away if anyone ask but she said the bucket can be picked later but where and he looked surprised and said my place 106 lergergergend and said but in less than 10 minutes after that it won't be food but and instantly left with no word and he quickly paid for the bucket and because they applauded very hard as she had said and he bought another bucket but they did not stop so he bought a third one and left by then 5 minutes hard gone and now with three buckets of food he jumped into his car and drove fast to his house 106 lergergergergend and as he approach he saw her still searching and screamed so hard that she stopped and laughed and had a squirt from the vagina for the first time now expecting 1 bucket and going back to be applauded he came out with 3 buckets but she looked sad and said just 1 for this are the others yours or but but he said my turn twice but half but then so she didn't object but said if we then maybe us become but meaning now we are fucking buddies because if you fuck three times then then you are fucking buddies if not in a relationship but he smiled and said what if 4 then but she instantly had a clit arousal and said my hard is clit with a k at the end meaning my hard is click at the end and get fourth bucket but maybe and he looked surprised and said maybe what thinking and she said i am a cleaner when my hard is clit with a k that's it finished phinisnto she laughed he looked lost and said okay for the first time like a little girl that she looked lost and cried once and said okay too then the tone changed from the gods to the i can make money with you fast in one week than i can in 2 months but she said but and quite now not knowing what these means said i can't i have to go back and he said 3 says worth of food we can raise 800 dollars money i get every 2 months and she had a hard clit but refused to say anything regarding that and said i am honesty and prefer nothing to do with this and he said i beg you look the troubles i went for you so you can go with me they don't in 1 minute we get the money and go but because he had refused so she said you mean like you now look because of that you must make others fail first to feel good about yourself but he remained silent and said i am bankrupt and it's either those or the house pointing at it now he realised that if he don't give her her share to carry she will refuse and said yours but these babies still mine but either go with me now either go or bye and literally walked away and mean it and picked a piece honestly and started eating and cursed so hard that she shits herself obviously because the rim is so loose it can't hold anything now this is the interesting part of this case now if she go back she will not be applauded but if she goes then she would still come back another day with another but the bet was that she make him cum and then give all the meat so that when they say he gave her big meat that the rim fell she will see who ate the meat wasn't you so how can my rim fell for something i did not eat you eat so you fall creating news for the local people as a joke but she took it literally and said i can this bet anymore but we can only do one more but i have to take a shower first for half the bucket or one full deep until ejaculated then go to my home straight with huge arousal now he could feel that aroused him knowing that who ever was setting him up was the same person so he said he who sets you up now is also aroused that he forgot to close the line to protect you what does this mean are you for sale instead he looked around as if listening for a while and said whatever and instantly took a big hammer from the groove box of the car and stood there saying to do or not to and what could be shall be and strike her hard in the head that she did not speak and or say anything and died then he said i was told to kill you if you refuse my bet but if you had said yes i was going to spare your life and cancel all bets give you al three buckets to feed everyone now if they don't get meat they know you got meat and will keep it our secret forever so that if god is listening he will come one day and say this is exactly what you did and everyone protected you now let's look at the facts one by one can we say that he had the right to kill her if we ask the council of creation what can be of him this is the answer he can be very strict and say i did for her she must have done the same for me but she refused now what can be of her from now on she had failed to understand that and as already predefined must die with one blow to the head at the death switch itself so that nothing registers or her have the chance to send a message to god for help that as a way to prove that humans guide themselves and as such no human will ever be able to crack this case unless he can read god's manuals and if he did by whose authority and if by god's authority then we found our savior but otherwise must be killed for its through the devil and must die the same way by a single blow to the heard before any of the people who didn't get meat are arrested for complicity now if we look at all complicated cases then you can see a pattern developing in that if they are satisfactorily solved then there must be a good chance that a god exist because the true facts are hidden from the human brain and as such only a god can solve this case but even if he did you must ask by whose authority and if by god's authority then this man is your leader to guide you through tough times but if not by god's authority then he can only be reading the devils manuals meaning he will destroy us all and must be killed the same way meaning one blow to the head at the death switch itself to avoid alerting the devil that humans are killing us and not send message to the devil now this is interesting because it says that not send a message to the devil let's look deeper into this if we ask what can be of humans without god this is what we get humans will be lost and can humans live with the devil alone the answer is no who wants darkness alone everyone wants a bit of both now what can be of humans without Yahweh darkness and death because the devil only do this to get everyone get killed while Yahweh wish that one of you finds him to know how to live forever on earth if not forever then for 10000 years alive in forever rejuvenating human bodies that take cycles to change see creation 089283486982348691028367892083210184869821006832109710 19 now if we ask what can be of humans alone this is the answer humans alone will be like a blind person leading another but now this test does it make sense can only an authorized person be of Yahweh now the only truth is that yes he must be endorsed by Yahweh himself and be in the books of creation at the centre stage with Yahweh himself on his right side replacing joseph and ann but superimposing them now what can be of the council of creation with a super human i mean the smartest person on earth to find Yahweh's image and know 20bcritical requirements and then pass all first with flying colors and then ask for Yahweh's permission the problem with humans is that there don't know how to talk to Yahweh ever so how can they ask him anything? now if we ask the court of creation what can be of humans and Yahweh together the dream of creation is fulfilled Yahweh judging those who have been killed and the other earthly god judging the killers within 40 days of death of the victim and 2 months punishment after 40 days and his or her death too within six months of killing someone else this will make everyone think twice before killing another especially horrific just to prove that god doesn't exist when he does just ask humans to whisper gdotodotd which is g.o.d [in davidgomadza god exist as his image and authorized but how davidgomadza is human oh my god he is authorized but how and by who? Yahweh himself authorized the clevest human being ever who understood what is needed and took all crowns alone without the angels help the angels are meant to guide humans towards being Yahweh but all 20 criteria met with the highest colors] now if we ask what could be of humans without their creator that means lost now let's conclude this case also as the shortest of all time and the most simplest because from start we have the same people who concludes the case as well horad blacksmith said today i want to fuck for free prostitutes finished all money without a single oh my god from my side damn it hurts i just wonder who is up to this women are now hard to get what's left are trash does anyone run a pimp circle because this month i will fail to pay the mortgage for the the first time in 20 years my wife susanna left me and i am thick hard cock it has been 3 months if i spent all money and i can't fuck 3 times i swear this bitch ends up in my garden forever that pit neighbor's have been complaining about closed and if they ask i will say did it up again and buy meat knowing that who ever digs it up will be hammered in the death butthole so he shit no death to anyone even the devil and tomorrow i will sell the house to that estate agent and go away forever now this is a man in distress the system has become so corrupt the women have become so clever that sex is so rationed he gad to be smart to get a little head in for all he had left with and all this in the eyes of the public reversing all good standard dating with pimping where the clock dictates ejaculated rather than good time something so dear that now he had to fail to pay mortgage rent to satisfy just seeing pussy or ass as he had become so hungry that who ever was behind this wanted him so horny that he rape someone so they have a job but he refused and said i will kill her so that god in the end will see that i am right when life has become like this the food then becomes the bait not the other way my dream is to let other men enjoy sex as it should be i will tell you a list of the police officers behind this the price of my house today has crashed to a quarter hence even though the woman i fucked and later killed is 22 years they will say they gave me a quarter to everyone a 14 year old to cover for their thieving of my house which was on the market for a whooping 270 000 which was a huge sum but with these prostitutes i lost everything i think they change

enzymes in my body from male to female because at times i have nothing down there meaning no energy testosterone is energy instead they put enzyme 2 for female and everyday one of them caress my breast until i feel like killing someone and they say we will give you someone to kill just wait a moment now today they caressed me all night for a man it triggers the need to kill ruthless without question and ask questions later and they said today we give you our finest because this one will send you to jesus and back i have 270 left i month mortgage and death of house if i don't give notice they repossess and sell at a quarter to the police what a house burglary in broad day light it hurts i cried i worked harder than everyone and learnt to avoid sex so i pay mortgage now because i am so good they tell everyone i can't cum after switching enzyme 1 for enzyme 2 which is progesterone if my doctor doctor astreet is right that means swapping male to female when i don't have money then female to male so they send their prostitutes for the money i refused for 3 months and now they leave enzyme 1 at full blasts the cravings to see just a moving vagina has incapacitated that now i have two choices to kill a vagina and be scared of it or to fuck it hard it tears if it does she must shit herself and if she does she won't go she will want to clean first if she agrees she must first give me one full round which i enjoy like never before and if i enjoy it then she will be willing to help me to get only one moths rent for the mortgage where other men can't cum and i will use my size to intimidate them into not cummings just dipping once and taking the money after that marry her forever if she refuse i will take her to court for prostitution on grounds she refused marriage but..
he stopped and said what if and stopped them for the first time his asm replied so loud he shit himself what if would be putting her in your position and ask the same question and her response would be if i say no he would ask me to marry me of which i agree but we lose the house which is just a vast and an obsession with price which the police would take at a quarter in exactly 2 months 20 days and 28 minutes and counting and host a reward after 20 years for those who have killed both of us if he is smarter if i refuse he will say marry me instead and borrow money from me and tomorrow i will sell the car and pay 6 months mortgage and have sex every minute

but...he cried because his asm was diverted to her when he shit himself now this is not just the shortest case but also the most traumatizing case of all time in the council of creation because both got killed same day same time having sex and buried same grave with all wishes but the house because all those applauding will benefit more if these lose the house now let's conclude by saying i cried watching everything unfold humans sometimes have real love watch this i love you but i know and your butts shelved in your butts literally who wants to growl like an animal and wake up everyone for a but when but can be a excuse me your butts have become so many that by definition but and but cancels out and what's lefts is that's the idea you thought i am so horny but i love you but you i know but but but in butt and growl for more butts now all offer butts for more butts then all cheer only to pick next but among them but you hooked on but oh i see my heart and legs shiver with but i know so i ran there and see you with no erection but so i said then but but they think you go to toilet with bucket for next to but and pick but you run for a but especially when rent is due as all had saved for the best deal in town but and poison and free house but you but oh i see i thought all but love you? but you joke too much the other day you but and then but i know i was but if i then but but if you and then can't the result be but only if i but but you but now when i come to town all but then i decided to but you surprisingly you but instead of marry me so all laugh and say but can't say because you but i only but to help and keep but you so why not say marry me but i am broke so i sell the house my father owns but died so mine with no mortgage and pay you half to pay your mortgage and say thanks for marrying me but now if you want we both but and all them they bu.tt so they stopped and he cried and said i said i am not the best but my heart loves you so she said after but your heart but so confess what's the but about he said instantly they said marry her then we kill you both and bury you in your own grave switch and live forever because you will lose what we want both houses for the police and she said bitch-holes so he proposed and they got married he said i but and she said but i and they fucked once she then said i but but but so he stopped and said but what and instantly the door opened and pc atnpsrteomn a man who had tormented them came while he is about to cum and said who gets the house when you both have died what you were supposed to do to her must happen to you and he hit him on his death switch that he died instantly she said i don't want anything i lost mine for his but take all don't touch my vagina i am pregnant and it's yours that rattled him and said i have a wife the idea is to bring up the child as helping you but it's his not mine get it harshly she looked confused and said but then stopped he only said but what before he struck her too but so hard that she miscarriages there and there and said what pregnancy but then the others came like pc artttop who help carry the bodies in a big hole in front of the house and said but what if then what instantly others came outside and said but the house belongs to us

they then said the house belong to but now even though we said it was the most easiest and simplest shortest case it looked at it become complicated later as pc antorop became the killer for he killed horad blacksmith and christine marie eastin

christine marie broadnton-blacksmith that lasted a week before pc antsprtsmonen struck both at death switch killing both before taking the house at a quarter the value they gave them and gloating about it they were both buried at coordinates 086677984838268798677854281086774892318600 in psteretstertst california in a pit dug buy the community who were denied meat or the local translation christine marie eastin electromagnetic wave number is 869877283898487128684828321084189012310083210748 now we can get horad blacksmith number but we have a way so his electro magnetic number is 869978382489018778321098776841092178432018678901249036 7109238900741638492066 his current location is 775588382489032778628098324890183267496874286670 which is below christine marie eastin but in same grave

the end.

the end

the claim

the reward offer

the collection

www.twofuture.world/donate

about david gomadza

visit www.twofuture.world

signed david gomadza
ask.davidgomadzaauthorised.licensed.checkya.askya.ya
17may23.25pm
scotland
00447719210295
davidgomadza@hotmail.com
info@twofuture.world
www.twofuture.world

www.ingramcontent.com/pod-product-compliance
Lightning Source LLC
Chambersburg PA
CBHW051408250726
48656CB00006B/2343

* 9 7 9 8 3 2 5 9 6 0 6 0 4 *